IMAGES
of America

WESTFIELD

Welcome to

WESTFIELD

The Best Town in U. S. A.

Postcard dated October 22, 1912. Postage was 1¢. (Barbara Bush Collection.)

IMAGES
of America

WESTFIELD

The Westfield Athenaeum

ARCADIA

First published 1996
Copyright © The Westfield Athenaeum, 1996

ISBN 0-7524-0451-2

Published by Arcadia Publishing,
an imprint of the Chalford Publishing Corporation
One Washington Center, Dover, New Hampshire 03820
Printed in Great Britain

Library of Congress Cataloging-in-Publication Data applied for

The original Westfield Academy building. The Westfield Academy, built in 1800, was modeled after Benjamin Franklin's academy in Philadelphia. It was the seventh school of its kind to be organized in Massachusetts. The doors opened on January 1, 1800, and the school was open to both young men and women on a tuition basis. The bell in the belfry was cast by Paul Revere. The original building was wooden and was located on Broad Street on land purchased from Aaron King. In 1859 it was moved to the back of the property. A new brick building was built which the town purchased in 1867 for $35,000. The citizens voted at a town meeting to petition the general court for a school charter. The town of Westfield put up a sum of 600£ ($2,000) for the purpose of erecting and supporting an academy. Additional money to finance this school was obtained from the sale of land that had been granted to the town by the General Court. This land was located in what is now the state of Maine, but at the time was still part of Massachusetts. The sale resulted in an additional $5,000 for the academy.

Contents

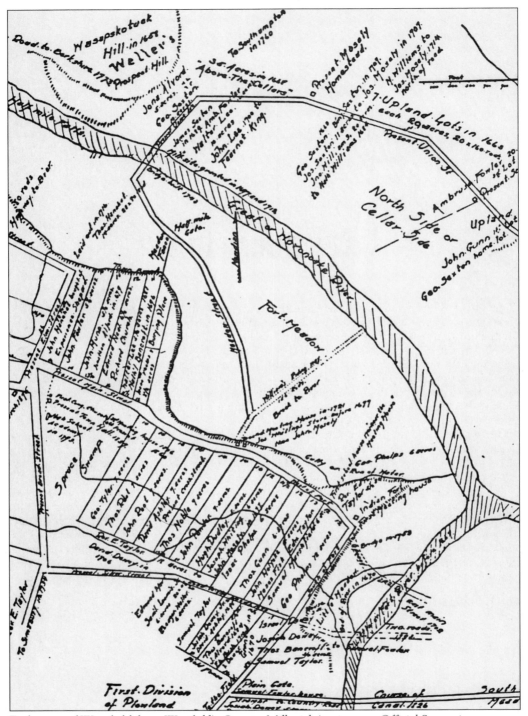

Early map of Westfield from *Westfield's Quarter Millenial Anniversary Official Souvenir*.

Introduction

The city of Westfield, Massachusetts, nestled at the foot of the Berkshires, was first settled in 1639 and was granted the status of township in 1669. What began as a farming community had, by the end of the nineteenth century, become an area of great industrial activity.

Along with the Industrial Revolution came an influx of newly arrived immigrants who settled in Westfield. They worked for growing businesses such as Stevens, the Crane Brothers, and Mars ; the United States Whip Factory, where most of the whips used in the United States were made; the H.B. Smith Company, a pioneer manufacturer of boilers and radiators; the Foster Machine Company, known worldwide for its textile machines; and the Westfield Manufacturing Company, maker of the Columbia bicycle.

During this time Westfield was home to Irish, Lithuanian, Polish, and Slovak immigrants, as well as the English, who had in some instances lived in Westfield for over two hundred years. As each new group emigrated to Westfield, its members integrated themselves into the community, but kept their heritage alive through gatherings at churches and social clubs.

This photographic essay chronicles the lives of the people of this community. We will see a picture of Westfield from its beginnings to the late 1960s. Authors Joan B. Ackerman, head of the reference department at the Westfield Athenaeum, and Patricia Thompson Cramer, director of the Westfield Athenaeum, have compiled this history from newspaper articles and histories of Westfield, the records and photographs of the athenaeum, the Western Hampden Historical Society, the Connecticut Valley Historical Museum, and private photograph albums donated or purchased by local residents, such as Barbara Bush and Ross Conner.

One

Around Town

Park Square, July 7, 1955. In the foreground is the statue of Major General Shepard, an early American patriot. The General William Shepard Monument was dedicated on September 3, 1913. Augustus Lukeman, a student under Daniel Chester French (one of America's most distinguished sculptors), designed the statue. It is standing with its back to the Green, facing Broad Street. The building on the right is the historic town hall, built in 1837. The first Westfield High School classes were held here from 1855 to 1868. (Barbara Bush Collection.)

The elms of Westfield, June 12, 1934. In the background is the First Methodist Church, which was built in 1875, demolished in 1967, and rebuilt in 1968. Note the Soldiers' Monument on the Green. It was erected in 1871 and the soldier was modeled after Captain Andrew Campbell, a member of the 46th Regiment of the Massachusetts Volunteer Infantry. The statue was designed by M.H. Mossman, also a member of the 46th, and was cast by the Ames Company of Chicopee. The statue commemorates the sixty-six men from Westfield who died in the Civil War.

Trolley car, *c.* 1915. The Westfield Street Railway System provided the town with transportation services for many years, beginning in the late 1800s with horse-pulled trolleys. When Woronoco Park opened in 1894, the Westfield Street Railway System refused to extend the tracks from Pine Hill Cemetery to the park, and a rival company was formed. In 1895 the tracks were electrified and the two street railway companies combined.

The Second Congregational Church and the Green, April 3, 1930. This photograph was taken from the Methodist church steeple. (Ross Conner Collection.)

Photograph taken from the Methodist church steeple looking down on Broad Street, April 3, 1930.

The Westfield Athenaeum on Main Street before the turn of the century. Emerson Davis developed the plan for the formation of the library, which was incorporated in 1864. Samuel Mather pledged the first $10,000 to the library and has been referred to as its founder. The second benefactor was Hiram Harrison, who gave the land together with a handsome brick and brownstone one-room building that he had built as the library. The athenaeum was later moved to the corner of Elm and Court Streets.

Noble Hospital, 115 West Silver Street, c. 1899. The hospital was dedicated on February 24, 1897. It was named after Reuben Noble, a native of Westfield and a prominent whip and cigar manufacturer and banker. Noble left one-third of his $130,000 estate for the establishment of the hospital, "for the reception of persons who may need medical or surgical treatment during temporary sickness or injury." The present hospital, located on the same site, was dedicated on October 15, 1958. (Ross Conner Collection.)

Number 67 Court Street, 1922. This house was built between 1894 and 1896 for Henry Taylor at a cost of $25,000, making it the second most expensive house built in Westfield at the time. Henry Taylor was a wholesale tobacco dealer. The building was once owned by the Knights of Columbus and is now part of the YMCA. (Ross Conner Collection.)

View along upper Court Street, 1922. The William Lyman house (foreground) at 81 Court Street was built in 1894 for $5,000. (Barbara Bush Collection.)

Men working on cobblestones on Elm Street. In the background are the First National Bank, Conner's, Chapman & Shine, the Opera House Block, and Crotty's Drugstore. (Ross Conner Collection.)

Elm Street, c. 1910. The First National Bank (now BayBank) appears next to Conner's. Note the trolley car and the soldiers on the truck. (Ross Conner Collection.)

Masonic Temple located at the corner of Elm and Chapel Streets. The elm tree fell as the result of a windstorm. The Westfield Savings Bank is now located on this site. (Ross Conner Collection.)

Franklin Street in winter. This view might depict Kelsey's Farm. (Ross Conner Collection.)

Ives Block. This building, which for many years stood at the corner of Main and Broad Streets, was torn down to supply a site for the former post office building. In earlier days, the Ives Block was counted as part of the famous "Rum Row." (*Westfield's Quarter Millenial Anniversary Official Souvenir.*)

Frog Hole, August 27, 1928. The filling station was affiliated with the Little River Inn on Route 20 at East Main Street and Little River Road. The station was owned by Herbert Pomfrey and is now the site of Little River Plaza. (Ross Conner Collection.)

Flood of 1936. This house on Little River Road is shown on March 19, 1936. (Ross Conner Collection.)

Corner of Main Street and Little River Road, c. 1899. At the corner of Little River Road and East Main Street was a hostelry called the Riverside Inn, owned by Harry Lamb. The tavern was first licensed to sell liquors and to entertain travelers in 1668. On the opposite corner was the Old Bray house, which was once a tavern. During the time Harry Lamb owned the Riverside Inn, he purchased the Old Bray house, demolished it, and built a house on the site. (Ross Conner Collection.)

Westfield State Sanatorium, opened February 16, 1910. Under a legislative act of 1906, a five-man commission was selected to choose a site "west of the Connecticut River for a State Hospital for consumptives." The site chosen was located on East Mountain Road. Dr. Henry Chadwick was the sanatorium's architect and first superintendent. In 1962, the name of the institution was changed to the Western Massachusetts Hospital. (Barbara Bush Collection.)

Westfield Town Farm, c. 1899. This site on Russell Road was home to Noah Clark's Inn until 1840. The town farm (also known as the poor farm) was established in 1841. (Ross Conner Collection.)

Westfield Waterworks, Tekoa Reservoir, September 7, 1907. (Barbara Bush Collection.)

Old Charles Reed place under the hill. This was the first house built south of Western Avenue. About 1858, two men were arrested here for making counterfeit coins. A few years later, the group moved their headquarters to a huge cave within rattlesnake-infested Mount Tekoa. Some residents investigated the cave and found the forge, anvil, and smelter used in making the money. A large stone slab was placed over the entrance by an unknown party, sealing it off forever. (Pitoniak's *Western Massachusetts History*.)

HORSE RACES

AT

Woronoco Park

Under the auspices of the

Bay State Short Ship Circuit·

Wednesday, Thursday and Saturday

JULY-21, 22 and 24

Nine Classes. Fastest Horses in the country.
Band Concerts each afternoon.

ADMISSION 50 CENTS

GRAND STAND 25 CENTS

EVERYBODY PAYS AT THE GATE

Woronoco Park advertisement. James Larkin, R.B. Crane, James Crane, R.D. Gillett, Ira Miller, and a few others formed a corporation to build a park in Westfield in 1893. The land chosen was approximately 2.5 miles from the Green and included the old Holland property on Western Avenue and a part of the boulevard called "Munn's Meadow."

Woronoco Park. Located on Western Avenue where Park Drive is now, the park consisted of a half-mile racetrack surrounded by grandstands and a pavilion housing entertainment and refreshments. Opening day on June 27, 1894, featured a hot air balloon launch, bicycle races, fireworks, and two days of trotting races. Admission to the track was 25¢. In 1913 a fire reduced the grandstand to charred rubble. Horse racing continued until 1915 using a second grandstand, which burned in 1918. Racing was revived in 1933 for a one-day event. (Pitoniak's *Western Massachusetts History*.)

Hampton Ponds, c. 1909. A geological survey in 1897 indicated that the Hampton Ponds area had once been covered by a glacial lake. Sands had been brought into the lake by the Manhan River, which is how the Hampden plains were formed. In the sheltered part of the basin, the sands surround the large depression of Hampden Pond. This depression is called Pequot Lake and the surrounding area is called Hampton Ponds. (Barbara Bush Collection.)

Hampton Ponds, c. 1909. The pavilion at Hampton Ponds was built in 1899 by Edmund Dupuis of Holyoke, who purchased the land from Lydia Searle. It was operated by the Lambert family for many years before being purchased by the state in the early 1970s. (Barbara Bush Collection.)

Tobacco field and barns. Westfield has had a long history in the growing, curing, and manufacturing of tobacco and tobacco products. For many years, especially in the late 1800s, tobacco finished a close second only to whips in dollar volume of products shipped from Westfield to all parts of the world. Westfield became known as one of the great tobacco centers of the Connecticut Valley. (Barbara Bush Collection.)

Atkins Dam on Moose Meadow Brook, near Pochassic Road, c. 1917. (Ross Conner Collection.)

Two
Faces from Our Past

Dancing class, *c.* 1930. (Connecticut Valley Historical Museum.)

Frances Fowler Dwight (1797–1886), sister of the Honorable James Fowler.

The Honorable James Fowler (1789–1873). Fowler married Lucy Douglas in 1820. An 1807 graduate of Yale College, he represented Westfield in the state assembly, was a state senator, and served on the governor's council. His home was on Court Street and is now the Boys and Girls Library of the Westfield Athenaeum.

Arthur Twing Schoonmaker, MD. Schoonmaker came to Westfield in 1895 from Springfield. He was the city physician for thirty-two years, was on the staff of the Noble Hospital, and worked closely with Professor Louis Allyn in his pure food and drug campaign. In addition, he aided in the development of the Westfield Board of Health and the Board of Public Welfare, and was a prime mover in the establishment of the Westfield State Sanatorium. This picture was taken on Bates Street.

Children of Dr. Arthur Schoonmaker, c. 1899. Schoonmaker was father to Hazel Edith and Ernest William. The Schoonmakers were the last family to live in this house, which became the permanent home of the Westfield Athenaeum in 1898.

Reuben Noble. Reuben was the son of Wills and Mary (Dewey) Noble. He was born in 1859 and died in 1928. He was married to Dr. Anngenette Fowler and was the father of Dr. Mary Noble. The early part of his life was spent farming and growing tobacco. In later years, he traveled extensively. The Noble home at 21 Noble Street is now owned by the Westfield Housing Authority.

Mary Noble, age three months. Mary was the daughter of Reuben and Anngenette Fowler Noble. Mary obtained a Ph.D. in law, taught at Rutgers, and then practiced law in Westfield.

Dr. Anngenette (Fowler) Noble with daughter Mary. Dr. Noble was the daughter of Josephus and Anngenette (Fowler) Fowler. She received a medical degree from the Women's Medical College in Maryland in 1893. She practiced medicine in Westfield for several years and served as president (1913) of the town's first parent-teacher association. In 1915 she was appointed a member of the town planning board, the first woman to serve on such a body in Massachusetts.

The Van Deusen family on an outing to Mount Tom. In 1911 Henry M. Van Deusen started construction on the Van Deusen Inn. Completed in 1913, it stood as a memorial to Van Deusen's career as a businessman and whip manufacturer. The inn burned down on January 6, 1936. Three houses owned by the Episcopal church are presently on the site of the former inn.

Bay State Cigar Company. The cigar company, owned by Charles Huber (left), was located at the rear of 16 Allen Avenue (Huber's home). Charles Huber's younger brother, Albert, is standing next to him. The manufacture of cigars started in Westfield in the 1840s. Cigar companies in Westfield manufactured cigars, plug tobacco, and snuff. Much of the tobacco used by local manufacturers was imported stock; domestic tobacco was largely used for binders.

Celebration of the Westfield State Sanatorium, 1912. From left to right are: Mrs. Eliza Rust Mosely, Agnes Gibbs, Eleanor Mosely, Loretta Gray, Rachel B. Allyn, Lewis B. Allyn Jr., Oretta Andrews, Philip E. Mosely, William Griswold, Clarence Brown, James Mather Mosely, and Fred Starr.

Charles Lloyd Austin, age three years, ten months.

Andrew Oleksak family, 1912. The Oleksak family home was on upper Western Avenue near the town line. (Pitoniak's *Western Massachusetts History*.)

Dr. James Holland. Holland was the son of Dr. James Holland and Lydia Stowe of Chester. Born in Westfield in 1815, he was a well-liked and respected local physician. He was a member of both branches of the Massachusetts Legislatures and served in the Civil War as a surgeon of the Manchester cavalry. He died on August 12, 1880.

Leonard Lafayette Knapp, Liza Hess Knapp, and children, c. 1895. Leonard L. Knapp was the grandfather of Arthur W. Knapp, retired president of Westfield Savings Bank.

Charles Tryon, *c.* 1902. Tryon was a
carpenter who boarded at 48 West Silver
Street.

Reunion of GAR (Grand Army of the
Republic) Veterans, 1922. (Ross Conner
Collection.)

Lou Herrick, *c.* 1898. Herrick was a student who lived at 17 Charles Street. He later became a teacher of French in Amherst. (Ross Conner Collection.)

Sample's Orchestra, 1924. From left to right are: Joe Sample, violin and band leader; Ruth Carroll, piano; Al Seher, banjo; Timmy Devine, drums; Ralph S. Conner, alto sax; Luther Allen, trombone; Leon Brezina, trumpet; and Bill Yelinek, trumpet. (Ross Conner Collection.)

Florence Barker. Barker worked as a clerk in Snow & Hayes, a dry goods store on the corner of School and Elm Streets. It is now known as Barney's Restaurant.

Veselak family. From left to right are: (front row) father Anton J., Marian (Haggerty), and mother Anna; (back row) Rose (Land), Julia (Carlin), Fred, Rudolph, George, Helen (Cacio), and Ann (Van Wart). Anton J. Veselak was born in Bohemia on January 16, 1876, and lived 102 years, 6 months, and 4 days. He was the owner of Veselak's Bakery on Meadow Street and was a beekeeper as well. He lived in Westfield for seventy-six years.

Anna Lusk and her sister. Anna, who died in 1934 at age eighty-five, was the widow of John Lusk. The Lusks lived on Jefferson Street. (Ross Conner Collection.)

Town hall firemen's muster, October 15, 1914. Pictured from left to right are: L. Steimer, G. Byers, P. Houghton, L. Fuller, J. Hyde, M. Toomey, H. Howard, P. Wall, A. Buschman, W. Marcoulier, H. Eaton, F. Ensworth, F. Snow, S. Conner, H. Randall, and two unknown persons.

City government officials, 1927. Included are: (front row) Fred Parker, George Searle, Louis Keefe, Harry Putnam, Harold Wittemore, and Homer Bush; (middle row) William Bagley, Louis Fuller, Joe Cullen, and Luther Hollister; (back row) Stan Healey and J. Chambers Dewey. (Ross Conner Collection.)

Westfield Athletics, 1923. From left to right are: (front row) Chet Lucia, Robert Rogers ("tap"), Henry Miller ("Heinie"), Ray Fitzgerald, and John Devine ("Skinny"); (middle row) John McGowan ("Mac"), William Barry ("Bill"), Alexander Sadowski ("Red"), Mr. King, George Davis ("Dixie"), Louis Clark ("Clicky"), and Lester Robinson ("Peanuts"); (back row) Arthur Green, James Burke, and James Lyon.

Italian group, 1921. By the beginning of the twentieth century, Italian immigrants were coming to Westfield. There was a community of Italians working and living at the Lane Quarry in the East Mountain Road section. Many who worked in the quarries later opened grocery and cobbler shops in the downtown area. The Italian community has several social and fraternal clubs that were organized by the immigrants. Saint Rocco's was opened in 1925 and the Italian Fraternal Society was formed at the same time. (Ross Conner Collection.)

Lithuanian group, 1921. The first Lithuanians came to Westfield about 1888. Many came to America because of cruel religious persecution in Lithuania. Saint Casimir's Society was formed in 1903 to provide aid to its members. It was through this group that Saint Casimir's Parish was established in 1915. Saint Casimir's Hall on William Street provided facilities for social events. The hall is now owned by the Sons of Erin, an Irish club in Westfield. (Ross Conner Collection.)

Slovak group, 1921. In 1884 Gregory Oleksak arrived in Westfield. He is believed to have been the first Slovak in Massachusetts. He worked on a farm in the Western Avenue section of town. A few years later, about two hundred Slovaks followed him to America, working in factories like Pope Manufacturing. Saint Stephen's Society was established in 1897 and instigated the movement to form a Slovak parish—Saint Peter's Church on State Street. The Slovak hall on East Silver Street is still a place for those of Slovak descent to meet.

Polish dancers, July 4, 1921. The first Polish immigrant, Tomasz Danek, arrived in Westfield in 1889. Most of the early Polish immigrants settled in the Meadow Street area. In 1902 the Saint Joseph's Mutual Benefit Society was organized. In 1903, the Holy Trinity Polish Roman Catholic Church was founded in an old whip factory on Elm Street. In 1920, a group of Polish people interested in the preservation of the Polish language organized Saint Joseph's Polish National Catholic Church on Main Street. (Ross Conner Collection.)

Minnie Kinard, 1931. Minnie's husband, Clarence A. Kinard, was the manager of the Westfield Gas & Electric Company. The couple's home was located on Hawthorn Avenue.

Dr. Irving Pomeroy and friends, 1907. Dr. Pomeroy is driving, and in the back seat are his brother, Lewis M. Pomeroy, and a friend from Gloucester.

Three
Places of Business

Marcoullier Brothers Lumber Company. This business was located at 44 Broad Street, c. 1925–1973. It is currently the site of the Lumber Center. (Ross Conner Collection.)

Northwest corner of Main and Mechanic Streets, c. 1921. From left to right are C.E. Bartlett's Wagon Shop and John Krach's Wagon and Auto Repair (later Healey's Garage). Bartlett's is now the site of Giguere's Used Appliances at 68 Main Street. (Ross Conner Collection.)

Main Street, c. 1920. Shown from left to right are: the Hampden Bank at 6 Main Street (formerly Jack's Clothing and now the Palczynski Agency); the Schermerhorn Fish Company at 10 Main Street; and the Lee Hing Chinese Laundry. Above the laundry was James Greenwood & Son, a shoe store. The Fleet Bank is now located at 10 Main Street. (Ross Conner Collection.)

Fred Schmidt Auto Agency, 47 School Street. This is presently the site of City Cleaners. Mr. Schmidt formerly sold buggies and carriages on the opposite side of the street.

Interior view of the Fred Schmidt Auto Agency. (Ross Conner Collection.)

Vitamin Food Company, *c*. 1928. The Vitamin Food Company was located at 38 Main Street in part of the U.S. Whip building. The building later became the Park Theater. (Ross Conner Collection.)

Number 6 Main Street, *c*. 1899. This building was formerly the Hampden Bank, later Jack's Clothing, and is now the Palczynski Insurance Agency. Buffington's Grocery Store (right) is now Fleet Bank. The Coleman Studio stairway leads to offices above the bank. (Ross Conner Collection.)

F.P. Rouette's motorcycle shop on Church Street, *c.* 1930. This building became the Strand Theater offices. Mr. Frank Rouette is the first man on the left on a motorcycle. This print was made from an old 8-by-10-inch glass-plate negative. (Ross Conner Collection.)

Rialto Theater on Elm Street, *c.* 1930–1940. Harold Farr is in the center with a hat and glasses. United Transmission is now located here. (Ross Conner Collection.)

Bryan Hardware Store, 59 Elm Street. In recent years, this was the site of Building 451; it is now vacant. (Ross Conner Collection.)

Interior view of the Bryan Hardware Store. (Ross Conner Collection.)

Front view of Conner's at 34 Elm Street, *c*. 1925. (Ross Conner Collection.)

F.F. Woolworth Store, 72 Elm Street, 1921. This site is now a vacant lot. (Ross Conner Collection.)

The Professional Building (64–66 Elm Street) Fire on January 6, 1952. (Connecticut Valley Historical Museum.)

View of the Professional Building after the fire, January 1952. The Van Deusen and Professional Building Fires both broke out on Sunday nights, sixteen years apart almost to the day. The two holocausts claimed a total of thirteen lives; seven died in the Van Deusen blaze and six in the Professional Building disaster. The latter fire, due to its size and location, proved to be the most startling and spectacular in the city's history. (Connecticut Valley Historical Museum.)

Arthur Mahoney Shop. This shop was located on Elm Street between the Gowdy Block and the Professional Building.

Elm Street, c. 1899. Brigham, Eaton & Co. at 108 Elm Street is now Down the Aisle Bridals. At 110 Elm Street were the YMCA building and the Palace of Fashion (later Moriarty's Shoe Store and now the Rhythm & Views movie theater and restaurant). Gladwin & Noble Brothers Hardware (later the Continental barbershop and now the Aspects and Walton Music Company) was at 120 Elm Street. Note the prices on the cobbler's sign. (Ross Conner Collection.)

Elm Street, *c.* 1899. Osborne Brothers City Market (116 Elm Street) is located at the far right. Lunch rooms and meals cooked to order are advertised above the store. (Ross Conner Collection.)

Poulin barbershop at 31 Elm Street, *c.* 1940. (Ross Conner Collection.)

Elm Street, c. 1900. Lambson & Rothery, house furnishers and undertakers, were located at 89 Elm Street. P.A. Payton's hair salon and baths were at 83 Elm, and Charlie Song's Chinese Laundry was at 81 Elm. Lambson Furniture is still located at 89 Elm. (Ross Conner Collection.)

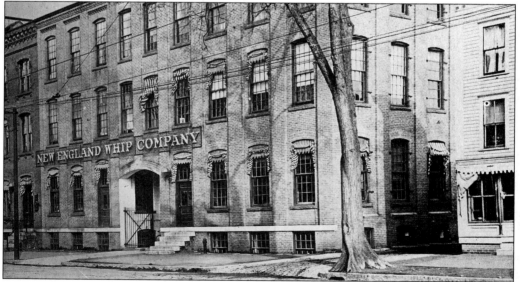

New England Whip Company at 165 Elm Street, c. 1884. The company was organized by Eugene and Daniel Doherty. Westfield was the center of the whip-making business, and by 1919 was known as the "Whip City" of the United States. This building later became the home of Robinson Reminders and finally was razed to make room for a parking lot and a Mobil gas station. (Ross Conner Collection.)

The Horton Grist Mill on North Elm Street by the Great River Bridge before 1894. The Horton Grist Mill was later moved to South Broad Street.

The Great Flood of 1878. This view looks south on Elm Street after the flood, showing the covered bridge. Two whip factories were wrecked in the flood, and a house on East Bartlett Street was carried east. On the left is a tenement house and the Johnson Organ Company. Across the river can be seen the water tower, switch house, and freight house of the Boston & Albany Railroad, as well as the Prospect Hill School.

Sterling Radiator on the east side of North Elm Street at Notre Dame on August 3, 1955. The 1955 flood was the granddaddy of all floods in this area.

Stevens Paper Mill and Dam, August 3, 1955. The flood was caused by Hurricane Diane, which left behind nearly 26 inches of rain.

J.W. Adams Nursery. In 1912, the firm of J.W. Adams moved to a farm of 40 acres in Westfield on East Main Street. This piece of land is now the site of a Wal-Mart store. (Ross Conner Collection.)

Lane Trap Rock Quarry, *c.* 1919. This quarry was started around 1894 by John S. Lane and his son Arthur. The first quarry site was located at the foot of the hill abutting Springfield Road and the Boston & Albany Railroad tracks near the Westfield-West Springfield line. This point is now known as Lost Lake, a popular swimming hole. About 1898, quarrying operations were shifted up the hill to their present site.

Four
People At Work

Noble Hospital nursing group, 1920. Note the bibs and cuffs. (Ross Conner Collection.)

Employees of the Bay State Cigar Company. The cigar company was located on 22 Arnold Street. One of the employees was Charles Huber who later (*c.* 1910–1915) purchased the company and had it moved to the rear of his home at 16 Allen Avenue. (Barbara Bush Collection.)

W. Warren Thread Works on South Broad Street. This company manufactured whip thread and spool cotton. It was opened by William Warren in a factory located opposite the railroad station. In 1898 the firm moved to South Broad Street. (Ross Conner Collection.)

Andrew J. Smith, Westfield whip maker, 1895.

Smith Feed Company, c. 1885. The feed company was located at 10 School Street and was owned by Edward D. Smith who lived at 27 Washington Street. It is now the site of the Good Table restaurant. Andrew Duris is on the right in the wagon, and Paul Cutler is on the left. In the background, third from the left, is Theo Smith.

Standard Oil Company truck, October 17, 1916. (Ross Conner Collection.)

Standard Oil Company of New York, c. 1915. Standard Oil was located at the rear of 98 Elm Street near the railroad. Harry Hammersley was the agent. He was also associated with the American Holly Whip Company. (Ross Conner Collection.)

Steam derrick working on the New York, New Haven & Hartford Railroad, 1918. (Ross Conner Collection.)

Westfield Gas & Electric employees, c. 1930. From left to right are: Ed Clair, Jess Wheeler (at top), Louis Johnson, Charlie Allen, Frank Clair, Doc Cummings, Ed Fredette, Pat Coleman, Dan Curran, John Moriarty, and Superintendent Ed Dustin. (Ross Conner Collection.)

Woronoco Bank employees, *c.* 1925–1930. At that time the bank was located at 99 Elm Street. It later relocated to Court Street. (Ross Conner Collection.)

Westfield Fire Department, Arnold Street headquarters, 1919. From left to right are: (front row) Paul Schoenrock, Harry Saltus, and Henry Yarmesky; (back row) Second Engineer William Clark, N. Wesley Spencer, and Chauffeur George C. Byers. The fireman were knitting socks and sweaters for the members of the American Expeditionary Forces in Europe.

Chatlos' Trucking Company Model T truck, 1920. Steven Chatlos, the owner, is pictured on the right. His business was located at 24 Hancock Street. (Ross Conner Collection.)

Chatlos' moving truck, 1920. The truck had to be cranked by hand to start. Mike Morris is pictured on left and Stephen Chatlos is on the right.

Picture of a still on Russellville Road during Prohibition. (Ross Conner Collection.)

Liquor made on Russellville Road in the days of Prohibition. (Ross Conner Collection.)

Sherman's Mill Bridge, 1920. In 1927 this bridge collapsed when a car ran into the side of it. It was reconstructed in 1928. (Ross Conner Collection.)

Sherman's Mill Bridge under construction, c. 1928. (Ross Conner Collection.)

O.B. Parks & Company, *c.* 1900. This company, located at 55 North Elm Street, was a dealer in groceries, flour, crockery, hardware, and agricultural implements. The site is now the location of Westfield Decorating.

Road oil truck on North Elm Street, 1917. (Ross Conner Collection.)

Veselak's Bakery and truck, 106 Meadow Street, 1926. Although no longer a bakery, this building is still located on the same site. (Ross Conner Collection.)

Outside S.S. Conner's stationery store, *c.* 1925.

R.S. Conner. Conner is standing in the alley behind S.S. Conner's. The alley was called Wesley Place. (Ross Conner Collection.)

Possibly John H. Phillip Carriage and Wagon Makers and Repairers at the rear of 11 Bartlett Street, *c.* 1925. (Ross Conner Collection.)

Employee of S.S. Conner's, standing at the back of the store. (Ross Conner Collection.)

Harry W. Hammersley, 1918. Hammersley served as the Westfield agent of the Standard Oil Company of New York. (Ross Conner Collection.)

Westfield Police Department, c. 1930. From left to right are: (front row) Patrolman J. McDermott, Michael F. Murphy, Captain William J. O'Brien, Chief Thomas F. Daley, Sergeant Michael J. Condon, Patrolman Michael J. Slattery, and Patrick Coffey; (middle row) Patrolman Archie Williams, Michael J. Daley, Anthony Michalek, William J. Rehor, and Michael J. Cummings; (back row) Patrolman George T. Hickson, Allen H. Smith, Edward J. Sheehan, and James J. Ashe. (Ross Conner Collection.)

Assessors office at Westfield City Hall, 1933. Seated are two members of the board of assessors: Chairman Herder C. Wood and Frank E. Tibbals. Standing behind the gentlemen is M. Elizabeth Martin, a stenographer in the assessors office in city hall.

Five

Claims to Fame

United States Whip Company. The whip industry began in Westfield in the early 1800s and grew by leaps and bounds. For more than 100 years Westfield led the world in the production of high quality whips and is still known as the Whip City today. By the turn of the century, the U.S. Whip Company did almost 85 percent of the whip business in the world.

Bay State Whip Company shares, 1893. The Bay State Whip Company was located at 287 Elm Street.

Beginning of whips in Westfield. The industry began when Joseph Jokes put a lash on a whipstock. Lashes were made of narrow strips of raw horse or cow hide plaited into cords, very much the same as they are at present. A piece of leather was rolled round, beveled to make the swell, and enclosed in the center. The lash was then rolled between blocks and varnished.

Plaiting room in the United States Whip Company's factory, 1911.

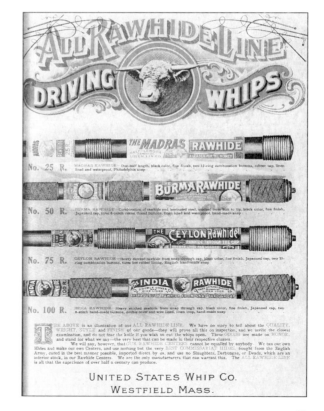

Page from United States Whip Company catalog. These samples represent the different kinds of rawhide whips that could be purchased from the United States Whip Company in 1911.

Edward Taylor. Taylor was the first minister of the First Congregational Church and was also known as the first American poet. Born in England in 1642, he came to America in 1668. After studying at Harvard, he reluctantly came to Westfield to serve the community. Reverend John Lockwood, a twentieth-century minister of the First Congregational Church, has said, "It is not our extravagant claim to assert that had he settled in Boston, instead of spending his life on the frontier, he would have been famous in the annals of colonial times."

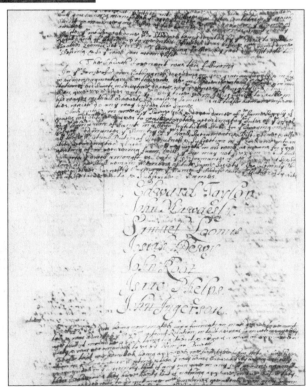

Church covenant. Note Edward Taylor's signature on this document.

General William Shepard (1737–1817). The eighty years of Shepard's life included service in the French and Indian and Revolutionary Wars. After the Revolutionary War, Shepard was chosen successively for state representative, senator, and councilor. He was elected to Congress three times. Shepard was a man esteemed by George Washington and was his companion in all the battles of the Revolution.

Major General William Shepard's house. Shepard's home was located on the corner of Franklin Street and Allen Avenue. His gambrel-roofed house stood on Franklin Street with the famous Shepard elm in front.

Richard Falley home at the foot of Mount Tekoa. Richard Falley was a master armorer who made muskets on the southeast slope of Mount Tekoa. Before the American Revolution he had built a hidden armory for the manufacture of muskets. The British authorities frowned upon this undertaking and tried to locate and destroy the armory, but had no success. The Falley home was burned in 1924 when a railroad locomotive set fire to Mount Tekoa.

William Johnson. Johnson was one of America's greatest organ builders. He began to manufacture church organs in 1844 at 273 Elm Street. The instruments produced by the Johnson Organ Company made excellent music in more than eight hundred churches. Some still survive today. This is a picture of a Johnson & Son Pipe Organ Opus #838 from 1896.

Door to the Landlord Fowler Tavern. The tavern was built in 1760. The original door can now be seen at the Metropolitan Museum of Art in New York City. It is about 8 feet high, 6 feet wide, and 4 inches thick. The door design was replicated when the tavern was made into apartments at 171 Main Street.

William Barnes' home. William Barnes was known as the "Copper King" of Westfield because he discovered a process of copper welding that was patented in 1907. He also developed a portable forge for the welding of electric trolley wires. The Barnes property on Western Avenue was sold to Stephen Oleksak, who built a sawmill on the site. (Pitoniak's *Western Massachusetts History*.)

Columbia bicycle, c. 1870. An "Ariel" is owned by the Edwin Smith Historical Museum of the Westfield Athenaeum.

Employees of the Westfield Manufacturing Company working on a Columbia bike, c. 1915. The company, now called Columbia Manufacturing, manufactured many popular bikes for recreation and played an important part in World War I. After being tested by government engineers, the Columbia bicycle was selected as the best bicycle for use by our troops abroad. Orders for over 35,000 military wheels were placed with the Westfield Manufacturing Company. Many thousands of these bicycles played an active part in the actual warfare at the front.

Colonel Albert Pope, 1900. The Pope Manufacturing Company (owned by Colonel Pope) began the American bicycle industry in 1877. The business started in Boston, moved to Hartford, and around the turn of the century it moved to Westfield, where it took over the Lozier automobile plant. It later became the Westfield Manufacturing Company and more recently the Columbia Manufacturing Company. The name Columbia has been used on bicycles since the beginning of the business.

Prof. Lewis B. Allyn, 1903. The chemical laboratory at the right was located at the Westfield State Normal School, where Allyn was head of the chemistry department. His "Westfield Standard for Pure Foods" gained the city fame as the "Pure Food Town." This nationally known list showed "the usual adulterations found in the average food product." Professor Allyn was murdered in his home by an unknown assailant on May 8, 1940. The crime has never been solved.

Loomis Model 1 Park Wagon, nicknamed the "Spider," 1899. Gilbert Loomis, a pioneer auto manufacturer and inventor, began his career in 1890 in Westfield, where he opened a bicycle shop and became a renowned bicycle designer and builder. A. Duryea, an automobile manufacturer from Springfield, provided him with the inspiration to build his own car. In 1903 the Loomis Automobile Company was sold to Samuel Squires of Westfield. Late in 1903 it was incorporated into the Pittsburgh Autocar Company.

Atwater Quarry, 1927. Westfield marble was at one time considered to have the best variety of color in the U.S. The city was especially famous for its serpentine marble. Examples of Westfield marble can be seen in famous buildings throughout the country, including the Empire State Building, Saks 5th Avenue, and Lincoln's Tomb. (Ross Conner Collection.)

Stanley Customer Catalog, 1957. Stanley Home Products began operation on August 15, 1931, in a tobacco shed in Westfield. It was started by Frank Stanley Beveridge to sell household and grooming aids. In 1938 the company moved to 42 Arnold Street and in the late 1960s built a new administrative building on Western Avenue. In 1996 the company sold its direct selling division to focus entirely on its gift division.

Frank Stanley Beveridge. The founder of Stanley Home Products is shown here with James Petrone, one of the company's original seven associates. (Connecticut Valley Historical Museum.)

H.B. Smith raising a stack from a coke pile, 1919. Brothers Henry B. and Edwin Smith founded the H.B. Smith Company in 1853. For some years the principal product of the foundry was ornamental fences, which were in vogue at the time. The Smith brothers also ran a lumber yard. In 1860 the business purchased the patent for the manufacture of a new sectional cast-iron boiler and indirect pin radiators. H.B. Smith became the pioneer manufacturer of cast-iron boilers and radiators. (Ross Conner Collection.)

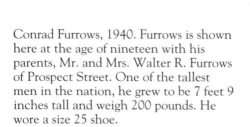

Conrad Furrows, 1940. Furrows is shown here at the age of nineteen with his parents, Mr. and Mrs. Walter R. Furrows of Prospect Street. One of the tallest men in the nation, he grew to be 7 feet 9 inches tall and weigh 200 pounds. He wore a size 25 shoe.

Six

Landmarks

Governor Ely's home on Broad Street, 1934. He was governor of Massachusetts from 1931 to 1935. This is now the location of the Governor's House, a nursing home. (Ross Conner Collection.)

Dewey house at 87 South Maple Street, built in 1735. The house museum is owned and maintained by the Western Hampden Historical Society. It was built for Jedediah Dewey sometime between 1715 and 1756. It is an example of the Georgian style and is considered architecturally to be one of the most important buildings within the city. (*Westfield Historic Building Book.*)

Captain John Bancroft house, Pochassic Street. This house was built in 1750 and was the second brick house built in what was then Hampshire County. Captain Bancroft was a wealthy farmer who earned the title of captain for his service in the French and Indian Wars. He was placed under house arrest during the Revolution when he was suspected of helping the English. It was later revealed that he had been selling secrets to the British throughout the Revolution. (*Westfield, Massachusetts 1669–1969.*)

Moseley homestead. This home was located on the corner of Moseley Avenue and Union Street and was built by Captain William Moseley in 1786. In later years, it was sold and moved out West. (*Westfield and Its Historic Influences 1669–1919.*)

Holland house. Located at 38–42 Court Street, this house was razed about 1875. It stood where the three brick houses owned by the Episcopal church are located.

Number 98 Court Street. Mrs. Mary Rood purchased this land in 1865 and built this octagon house. Mr. H.B. Smith added the ell and built the third story in 1869. He also added the piazzas with iron fences cast by H.B. Smith Company Foundry. He sold the house to Lewis Lee in 1888, who sold it to Mrs. Emma Crowsin, who in turn sold it to Howard Noble in 1911. The house burned down in 1949.

Interior view of Clara Louise Kellogg's house at 43 Court Street, 1895.

James A. Lakin residence at 91 Court Street. It was built in 1899. Lakin was president of the Woronoco Street Railway Company and the Operaphone Manufacturing Company.

Number 180 Main Street, *c.* 1899. Owned by Frank Firtion at one time, this house is important to the community because it is the earliest known example of the Dutch Colonial Revival style in Westfield. (Ross Conner Collection.)

Ice fountain on the Green, winter of 1879. The man is Judge H.B. Parker, whose home was located at 45 Broad Street.

The General Shepard elm, 1898. This tree was located at General Shepard's home, which is now the corner of Franklin Street and Allen Avenue. It is believed that General George Washington once stood under this tree.

First Congregational Church, 18 Broad Street. The current church was erected in 1860. It has been remodeled several times but the original style and lines were kept.

Steeple of the First Congregational Church. On February 27, 1886, the spire of the First Congregational Church broke off above the clock in a heavy windstorm and fell into the sanctuary.

James Fowler home, 1895. This building stood on the corner of Elm and Court Streets and is now the Westfield Athenaeum. When the athenaeum building on Main Street became too small, there was an attempt to purchase the Fowler home. Unfortunately, that attempt failed. In 1898, the trustees of Westfield Academy "voted to convey as a gift the Fowler home, land and building without any consideration therefor" to the athenaeum. Additions were added in 1927 and 1966.

The 1927 addition in progress at the Westfield Athenaeum. (Ross Conner Collection.)

Landlord Fowler Tavern, 171 Main Street. This tavern was built about 1755. In 1761, Daniel Fowler was granted a license for the tavern, which functioned as an inn until the 1830s. From 1885 to 1916, H.C. Shaefer owned the property and conducted a cigar-making business on the premises. The tavern has been restored and converted into apartments. It has been judged eligible for inclusion on the National Register of Historic Places.

Clapp Tavern at 53 Court Street. The house was built for Ezra Clapp sometime after 1743. It originally stood at the corner of Elm and Court Streets. From about 1766 until the 1790s it was used as a tavern. During the American Revolution it was used to lodge soldiers. In 1825, James Fowler moved the tavern west to 53 Court Street. When Judge Homer Stevens lived in the house, dormers were added and the central chimney removed. It currently houses offices. (*Westfield Historic Building Book.*)

Sackett Tavern, 1259 Western Avenue. This structure was built about 1776 for Stephen Sackett. The tavern was sold to Titus Atwater, who operated it as a posting house. It remained in the Atwater family until it was purchased at auction by Matthew Pitoniak in 1900. For a long time it was called the Washington House because it was believed that General Washington stayed here, but there has never been any evidence to support this. In 1962 the tavern was purchased by Mr. and Mrs. William A. Fuller, who had it restored. (*Westfield and Its Historical Influences 1669–1919.*)

Westfield house, *c.* 1900. The Westfield house became the Elm Park Block at 29–33 Elm Street. It was located was across the street from Conner's stationery store.

Foster House. Located at 50 North Elm Street, this building was built in 1843 by Micajak Taylor. In the 1850s it was known as the Pontoosic House, but has had the name Foster House since the 1890s. It is a well-known restaurant today and is believed to be the oldest continuously operated tavern in western Massachusetts.

Hotel Bismarck, 16 Union Avenue. The hotel was built in 1899 by a very successful businessman, John Buschmann, and his son Thomas. It contained sixty rooms, thirty-seven of which were used for sleeping. There was an ornate roof garden where guests could enjoy meals and drinks while watching vaudeville acts or listening to an orchestra. The hotel closed in the 1930s. The building currently houses the U.S. Line Company, which manufactures fishing equipment.

Old Woronoco House as it appeared during the middle of the nineteenth century. Located on Elm Street, the structure was later called the Wilmarth House until 1886, when its name was changed to the Park Square Hotel. To the right was Brown's riding stable and on the left was Morse's Jewelry Store.

Park Square Hotel and Fred Schmidt's livery stable, c. 1898. In 1914 the hotel was remodeled and called the New Park Square Hotel. It burned down on December 11, 1942.

Van Deusen Inn, 1915. This inn was located on Court Street on the present-day site of three small houses owned by the Church of the Atonement.

Van Deusen Inn Fire, January 9, 1936. This fire was deemed the worst in the city's history. Seven people died and seven others were injured. Henry Van Deusen, a seventeen-year-old high school senior, and George Alexander, his grandfather, both died in the blaze.

Grandmother's Garden on Smith Avenue. In 1929 Albert E. Steiger presented Westfield with land for a public park with the hope that a part of it would be set aside for a colonial garden in memory of his mother, Mary Steiger ("Grandmother Steiger"). In 1934, Grandmother's Garden came into existence. In 1994 the city voted to close the garden due to a lack of funding. A Friends of Grandmother's Garden group was formed, and under its direction the site is being brought back to life.

Carillon Tower in Stanley Park. The tower was dedicated in the interest of peace and understanding among the peoples of the world. It was made possible through the gifts of thousands of people. It is located in beautiful Stanley Park, a showcase of natural beauty with rose gardens, waterfalls, footpaths, picnic sites, and many other attractions. The park was donated by Stanley Beveridge in 1949.

Seven

School Days

Westfield High School Orchestra, 1881. From left to right are: (front row) Eugene Greene, Joseph Beals, and Robert Gowdy; (back row) Stanton Conkling and Frank Fay.

Little River School on Little River Road at the curve where Shaker Road begins, *c.* 1885. This school is now a private residence.

Old Westfield High School on Broad Street, *c.* 1858. The original Westfield Academy building can be seen in the rear.

Westfield schools, *c.* 1919. At the top left is the Green District School, on the right is the Ashley Street School, and at the bottom is the Abner Gibbs School. The principals of these schools at the time these pictures were taken were, respectively, Clara Fitzpatrick, Ida C. Ashley, and Frederick Scott.

Westfield schools. At the top left is the Normal Training School (now the district court on Washington Street), on the right is the State Normal School (now the city hall), and at the bottom is the Fort Meadow School. At the time these pictures were taken, George Winslow was the principal of the Normal Training School and Mary A. Long was the principal of the Fort Meadow School.

Miss Anna Root. Anna graduated with the Westfield High School Class of 1903 and became a music teacher.

Westfield High School Class of 1903. From left to right are: (front row) Mabel Edgely, unknown, Bess Carroll, and Charlotte Lewis; (second row) Dick Ensign, unknown, Lillian Russell, Kitty Byers, George Clark, Susan Reed, Alice Brown, Mabel ?, and Vera Simpson; (third row) Robert Klar, unknown, Cecil Barber, ? Avery, ? Thomas, Ed Cadwell, unknown, Nettie Furrows, Irene Sauter, and Mary Harr; (fourth row) F.B. Schmidt, George Keefe, William Buschman, Charles Keefe, Lucy Lockwood, Susan Phelon, Ray Sanford, Bob Pease, Anna Root, Elizabeth Bush, Bertha Camp, Jim Miller, and Val Skiff. Notice the girls holding whips.

Westfield Trade School, 1913. Standing second from the right is Robert A. Dowling, who was the shop teacher until 1946.

Westfield High School Class of 1915 reunion, June 21, 1950. From left to right are: (front row) Ethel Dickinson, Moses Saffer, Margaret Sears, George Roraback, John Roache, Carl Flinn, Robert Emerson, W.A. Farmer, Pat Riley, Margaret Burns, and T.W. Bowler; (back row) Fannie Sadek, Ken Morley, Anna Lilis, Melven Coburn, ? Lucia, Josephine Regan, Fred Williams, Sarah Damon Long, Agnes Sullivan, Genevieve Pratt, Fred Ensworth, Mary Fallon, Chet Lucia, Ken Mallison, Blanch Carr, and James O'Rourke.

Normal School basketball team, 1919–20. (Connecticut Valley Historical Museum.)

Westfield High School Class of 1920. Members of the class were as follows (names not in corresponding order): Margaret Avery, Ed Bike, Elizabeth Cash, James Denman, Carl Bowers, Gertrude Devine, Mildred Beaks, Minnie Buschmann, Agnes Corcoran, Julia Dreisow, Earl Fowler, Doris Griffin, Irene King, Ruth Lincoln, Dorothy Horwood, David Little, Mildred Gordon, Elizabeth Hyde, Sophia Levine, Francis Lynch, Louise Mahoney, Emily McCormick, Arthur Phelps, Stanton Phelps, Richard Morrissey, Gladys Phillips, Rose Martin, Hazel Osborne, Mildred Phelps, Emily Pomeroy, James Powers, Walter Sponagle, Marjorie Stiles, Elmer Taylor, Irene Skelly, William Waters, Harold Rockwell, Eileen Stanley, Mary Swayne, Dana Turner, Catherine Tobin, Ruth Watson, Isabel Wood, Avola Banks, Sophie Blascak, Henry Borowsky, John Cavanaugh, Louis Gendreau, Louise Kobena, Edith Holcomb, Elizabeth Levie, Andrew Pallo, Hazel Sponagle, Kathryn Sullivan, Elizabeth Holcomb, Charles Orth, Emma Snyder, and Marguerite Welch.

Saint Mary's Grammar School graduating class, possibly 1921. (Ross Conner Collection.)

Abner Gibbs graduating class, 1923. (Ross Conner Collection.)

Prospect Hill graduating class, 1926. (Ross Conner Collection.)

Moseley School graduating class, 1928. (Ross Conner Collection.)

Girls' hockey team, 1929. Members of the team are as follows (names not in corresponding order): Captain Mary E. Lee, Manager Beulah Marcoullier, Coach Ethelyn Perceval, and team members Gladys Anderson, Leona Champagne, Margaret Chapman, Agnes Clancy, Alice Dineen, Annie Donald, Mary Gillett, Katherine Howard, Eleanor Lee, Ruth MacBrian, Mae Manning, Anna Orint, Marjorie Packard, Fay Peasley, Dorothy Richardson, Mary Risko, Edith Rogers, and Frieda Stiles. (Connecticut Valley Historical Museum.)

Saint Mary's basketball team at the Boston & Albany Railroad. The team was on its way to Glen Falls, New York, to compete in the annual Scholastic Basketball Tournament. Those who made the trip were as follows (names not in corresponding order): Reverend Florence S. Donohue, Coach John Houlihan, Captain O'Rourke, Manager Moore, and players Schoenrock, Devine, Siska, Grubert, O'Day, Halloran, Martin, Bryndza, and Conway. (Ross Conner Collection.)

Old high school on Broad Street, 1930. This photograph was taken from the Methodist church steeple. (Ross Conner Collection.)

Westfield State College's Dickinson Hall, King Street, in 1920.

Eight

Transportation

Mr. and Mrs. Frank Morse of 49 Jefferson Street. Mr. Morse was an undertaker for Lambson and Rothery, *c.* 1900.

Port of Westfield. For over fifteen years the basin of Westfield Harbor was located where the H.B. Smith Company buildings stand. A canal beginning in New Haven, Connecticut, passed through Westfield on its way to the Connecticut River at Northampton. The first excursion trip left from Westfield on November 1, 1829. The canal was in active operation until about 1847, when railroads became the preferred mode of transportation.

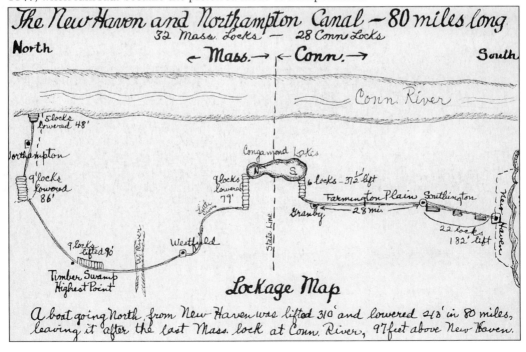

The New Haven and Northampton Canal – 80 miles long
32 Mass. Locks — 28 Conn. Locks

North ← Mass. → ← Conn. → South

Conn. River

5 locks lowered 48'

Northampton

9 locks lowered 86'

9 locks lifted 90'

Timber Swamp Highest Point

W. River

Little River

Westfield

Congamond Lakes
N S

9 locks lowered 79'

6 locks – 37½' lift

Granby

Farmington Plain   Southington
28 mi.

22 locks 182' lift

New Haven

State Line

Lockage Map

A boat going North from New Haven was lifted 310' and lowered 213' in 80 miles, leaving it after the last Mass. lock at Conn. River, 97 feet above New Haven.

First horsecar in Westfield. This car was owned by the Westfield Street Railway System. The horsecar tracks were electrified in 1895.

Westfield Fire Department hose carriage, 29 Arnold Street, 1903. We do not know who the fireman was, but the horses were Prince and Duke.

Standard Oil Company sleigh, *c*. 1915. This photograph was taken at the rear of 98 North Elm Street near the railroad.

Westfield Police Department, *c*. 1930. Third from the left is Archie Williams, by the cruiser is Chief Daley, and inside the sidecar of the motorcycle is Bill Rehor. (Ross Conner Collection.)

Woronoco Street Railway cars on Elm Street, 1890. Note the dirt road. (Ross Conner Collection.)

One of the last street railway cars, 1931. Note the miniature golf sign in the background. (Ross Conner Collection.)

Cowles Bridge, South Maple Street, 1907. The bridge was named for the Cowles family that lived just south of it on the west side of Southwick Road in the first part of the nineteenth century. This bridge was torn down to make room for a modern concrete structure.

Upper Crane's Mill Bridge, April 1917. Crane's Mill became Steven's Paper Mill in later years. (Ross Conner Collection.)

On the river. This view shows the Westfield River Bridge and dam. The Westfield Dye Works is on the far left and the original Johnson Organ Company is in the center. (Ross Conner Collection.)

County Bridge, November 1932. (Ross Conner Collection.)

Depot Square. This station of the Boston & Albany Railroad, on North Elm Street, became the Iron Horse Furniture Store in the 1960s. It was recently converted to an office building.

Roundhouse of the New York, New Haven & Hartford Railroad, 1894.

Depots, *c.* 1910. The New York, New Haven & Hartford Railroad station is on the left and the Boston & Albany station is in the center. The switching tower is on the right. (Ross Conner Collection.)

Westfield train station, possibly 1920s. Notice the policeman handcuffed to the man standing next to him. (Ross Conner Collection.)

First airplane lands in Westfield, July 13, 1914. The pilot was Jack McGee from Pawtucket, Rhode Island. He was flying a Burgess-Wright model biplane.

Franklin air-cooled roadster and a Curlee Clothing Co. airplane at Barnes Airport, 1926. (Ross Conner Collection.)

First airmail sent from Westfield, May 19, 1938. The load weighed 52 pounds and contained over 4,000 pieces of mail.

Barnes Airport Control Tower dedication, September 15, 1940. Barnes has been in existence since 1928 and has been municipally owned and operated since 1936. (Ross Conner Collection.)

World War I tank displayed on the Green, 1919. (Ross Conner Collection.)

Admiral Byrd's snow cruiser, *c.* 1939. (Ross Conner Collection.)

Nine
Celebrations

Christmas, *c.* late 1800s. This Victorian Christmas would not be complete without gas lights, a paper mantle, a tree, candles, clothes, cards, and presents. (Ross Conner Collection.)

May 3, 1911. This May Day celebration centered around the Civil War statue on Court Street.

Looking north on Elm Street in the center of town, 1913. The Morrissey Block is on the right. Note the "Woodrow Wilson, Thomas Marshall for President" banner hanging across Elm Street. (Ross Conner Collection.)

Boy Scouts on Decoration Day, May 3, 1917. (Ross Conner Collection.)

Camp Bartlett, 14th Infantry encampment in World War I, 1917. Camp Bartlett was opened on August 17, 1917, in connection with the mobilization of New England National Guard units. It was in operation for fourteen weeks, and thirteen thousand men were encamped here. On August 26, Camp Bartlett was visited by 100,000 persons, the largest crowd in the Westfield's history.

Westfield's 250th anniversary celebration, 1919. Note the banner across the road.

Westfield's 250th anniversary celebration, 1919.

Westfield's 250th anniversary celebration, 1919.

Westfield's 250th anniversary parade. Wednesday, September 3, 1919, was the last day of the Westfield celebration. Twenty thousand people braved a terrible rainstorm to watch the passing of the military parade. More than one thousand people marched, including two hundred women. This is the second section of the Red Cross, which included fifty young women carrying an immense Red Cross flag.

Westfield pageant at Wolf Pit Meadows September 1, 1919. This picture shows part of the audience. Wolf Pit Meadows was a recreational area on the flats between the Upper and Lower Crane Mills. It extended as far down as present-day Mill Street.

Community dancing and carnival during the anniversary celebration, Thursday, September 4, 1919. The minuet, which featured a group of sixteen young women dancing in pairs, was the closing dance of the evening. The pairs were as follows: Laura Junior and Frances Manning, Rena Manning and Barbara Hedges, Marjorie MacWorthy and Zilpah Meyer, Alfreda Mayor and Vesta Gannett, Ruth Harden and Ruth Wood, Catherine Wesson and Maude Hilmuth, Marion Brown and Mildred Beals, and Ruth Beals and Ruth Taylor.

"Seneca Wigwam," Mohican Forest, c. 1916. Joseph DuPort published the *Woronoco Valley Calumet* at his Mohican Press on Russell Road. The Seneca Wigwam, headquarters of the *Calumet,* was on the ancient hunting grounds of the Algonquin Indians—the Woronoakes.

International Order of the Red Men, July 1920. (Ross Conner Collection.)

Fourth of July parade, 1920. (Ross Conner Collection.)

American Legion float, Fourth of July parade, 1920. (Ross Conner Collection.)

High wheeler in the Fourth of July parade, 1920. (Ross Conner Collection.)

Apremont Day parade, 1927. This celebration was held in honor of a World War I regiment from Westfield that fought in Apremont, France. Edgar Gillett is on one of the horses. (Ross Conner Collection.)

Italian parade, Saint Rocco's Day. This photograph was taken from the New York, New Haven & Hartford Railroad bridge. (Ross Conner Collection.)

Westfield GAR Civil War veterans, Memorial Day 1922. From left to right are: ? Smith, unknown, ? Snow, unknown, Jim Noble, ? Belden, unknown, unknown, ? Douglas, unknown, unknown, unknown, unknown, ? Bartlett, Charles Farnham, and George Miner. Harry Cowles is in the background on the right.

Westfield Athenaeum Class of 1924. From left to right are: (front row) Sally Sector and Freda Cady (Morris); (back row) Lucy Holt, Howard Wooster (librarian), and Ruth Hubbard (Fink). (Ross Conner Collection.)

Telephone exchange Christmas party, 1927. Included are: ? Sherman, Ann Sathory Poulin, Elizabeth Barry, Jane Boakes, Helen Kelley, Rene Pendleton, Oliver Miller, Erma Leiegang, Josephine Folta, Jane Fitzgerald, Helen Lynch, Maude Fowler (sitting), Laura Whitney, Lillian Fairbrother, Josephine Plankey, Mary Sathory Rutzen, Alice Curran, Mae McDonald, Florence Gannon, and Florence Harray. The children pictured are unknown. (Ross Conner Collection.)

Wedding of John and Mary E. Miller, c. 1920. (Connecticut Valley Historical Museum.)

The 250th anniversary of the Get Together Club. This gathering was held at the home of Mr. and Mrs. Frederick L. Parker at 91 Court Street on January 25, 1926. From left to right are: (front row) L.B. Allyn, ? Patterson, George Gaylord, Reverend R.K. Smith, Chester Stiles, C.K. Prince, and Fred Parker; (middle row) Joseph Kenyon, ? Rothery, C.J. Little, Reverend W.S. Ayers, E.G. Clark, George W. Winslow, Kevin ?, Frank Grant, Harry Lane, L.C. Parker, R.C. Parker, George W. Miner, and Dr. C.B. Wilson; (back row) possibly Reverend Roy Myers, Joseph B. Ely, F.W. Bryce, possibly A.D. Robinson, Fred Goodwin, C.B. Warren, Dr. Chadwick, ? Kitredge, Burton Prince, George Roe, William F. Lyman, Harry Bradley, Leigh Sanford, and Dr. Miles Chisholm.

The 300th anniversary
parade, 1969.

The 300th
anniversary parade,
1969.

The 300th anniversary birthday cake on the Green, 1969.

Tercentennial celebration, 1969. In the back seat is George Searles, the first mayor of Westfield. Driving the car is Miss Barbara Bush.